Word Building for Infants

By

Cheryl .M. Greenidge

This book is dedicated to my daughter, Cheryse Greenidge, who attended the St. Martin's- Mangrove Primary School and went on to the Christ Church Foundation Secondary School where she gained a Barbados Scholarship in 2014.

First edition 2015
Second edition 2017
Cover design by Todd Forde
Edited by E. Jerome Davis
Published by Cheryl .M. Greenidge

ISBN   10: 1511765356

ISBN   13: 97 8-1511765350

ABOUT THE AUTHOR

Cheryl Greenidge attended St. Martin's Girl's School, the Princess Margaret Secondary School and the Barbados Community College. In 1988, she started her career as a primary school teacher. In 1997, she enrolled at the Erdiston Teacher's Training College where she completed her Diploma in Education. In 2005, Cheryl was made Early Childhood Coordinator at the St. Martin's - Mangrove Primary School. Cheryl's years of experience in the infants' department have greatly assisted her in compiling the material for this book. She is the author of 'A Spelling and Reading Aid for Beginners' and 'Grammar Made Easy for Infants' – Books 1,2,3 and 4.

CONTENTS

Part 2
Word family   Pages

Revision 2   55

Write the words in the correct box.

Write the missing letter. Copy the word.

Write the word in the box. (word puzzles)

Preface

After teaching my daughter, Cheryse, to read from the age of two and teaching the four to six age-group classes for several years, I was inspired to produce this word building book of word families. It is hoped that this book will enhance reading for beginners through word building and repetition of the words.

In this two part book, I have utilized twelve word families in different ways. These include matching the picture to the word, writing the word for the picture, writing the beginning, middle or ending letter for the word, rhyming words, word searches and choosing words to complete sentences. I have also included two test papers.

I believe that the use of this book will result in a progressive improvement in reading. It should therefore, be a helpful tool for both teachers and parents.

X

Part 1

✿ Match the picture to the word.

rat

bat

hat

fat

cat

mat

❀ **Write the word for the picture.**

bat   mat   rat   hat   cat   fat   vat

....

....

....

....

....

....

✿ Match the picture to the word.

can

van

tan

fan

man

pan

4

✿ Write the word for the picture.

pan   man   van   ban   tan   can   fan

....

....

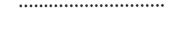

....

....

....

....

✿ Look for the words in the boxes and circle them.

Example:

cat	k c a t w d y s n

rat	m k c n r a t u f

fat	o s h f a t l c q

mat	r e m a t l c b s

hat	y p s o g b h a t

bat	k s b a t v l e x

✿ Look for the words in the boxes and circle them.

| fan | s r f a n e h c k |

| man | c y w m a n o z b |

| tan | f v t a n r h l s |

| ran | u r a n y t x m o |

| van | e t w o s f v a n |

| pan | p a n c o n e g k |

✿ Match the picture to the word.

pen

men

hen

den

then

ten

✽ Write the word for the picture.

ten   den   men   pen   hen   then   when

....

✽ Copy each sentence and put in the word for the picture.

1) He   has   a   little   .

....

2) Look   at   the   two   .

....

3) The   has   no   eggs.

....

✿ Match the picture to the word.

wet

net

vet

pet

set

jet

10

✿ **Write the word for the picture.**

set   net   vet   pet   wet   jet   get

....

....

✿ **Copy each sentence and put in the word for the picture.**

1) My 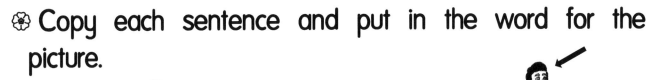 is at the   .

....

2) The  is  .

....

❀ Look for the words in the boxes and circle them.

hen	k c r t w d h e n
men	m e n p k a d u f
pen	o s h f a p e n q
ten	r f t e n l h b s
then	y k s o t h e n j
when	k w h e n v l b x

Look for the words in the boxes and circle them.

pet	w a u p e t h c n

set	c y w y o n s e t

net	n e t r w j i x n

wet	u k l c b w e t o

jet	m t j e t f h w n

get	p g e t o n z a k

✿ Match the picture to the word.

bun

nun

fun

run

sun

gun

14

✿ **Write the word for the picture.**

run   bun   fun   sun   pun   nun   gun

....

....

✿ **Copy each sentence and put in the word for the picture.**

1) Look   at   the    .

....

2) The   boy   eats   a   🍔 .

....

✿ Match the picture to the word.

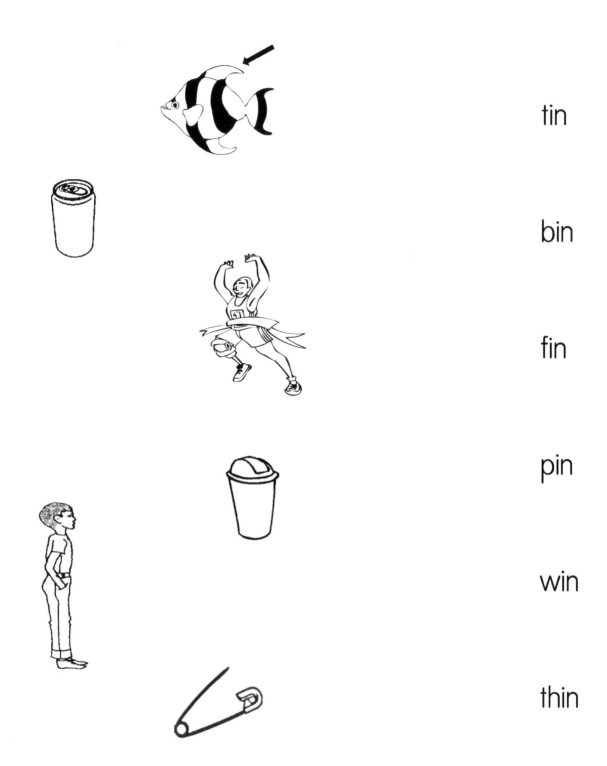

tin

bin

fin

pin

win

thin

✿ **Write the word for the picture.**

fin   win   pin   tin   sin   bin   thin

....

✿ **Circle a word from the brackets to complete the sentences.**

1) The fish has a little (win   sin   fin).

2) Put the (tin   sin   thin) in the bin.

3) Do not stick me with that (bin   tin   pin).

4) Can he (fin   win   bin) the race?

✿ Look for the words in the boxes and circle them.

| fun | k c f u n d y s t j h |

| bun | m k c z b u n p f s d |

| run | o q h s p t l c r u n |

| gun | r e m k t l g u n b c |

| nun | y t n u n b o f t q w |

| sun | x y t b t v l e s u n |

Look for the words in the boxes and circle them.

sin	g a t s i n h c w o g

| win | c y w i n d o z b r t |

| pin | p i n r w b h x l v a |

| bin | u d e q a h x m b i n |

| tin | e b w o s t i n m f k |

| fin | p s f i n o j a k z t |

Revision 1

✿ Write the words in the correct box.

bat   tan   rat   man   cat

fan   fat   ban   vat   can

at

an

22

✿ **Write the words in the correct box.**

net   ten   wet   den   jet

pen   get   then   set   when

et

en

✿ **Write the words in the correct box.**

run   fun   fin   win   pun

bin   sin   thin   gun   nun

in

....

....

....

....

....

un

....

....

....

....

....

✿ Write the missing letter and copy the word.

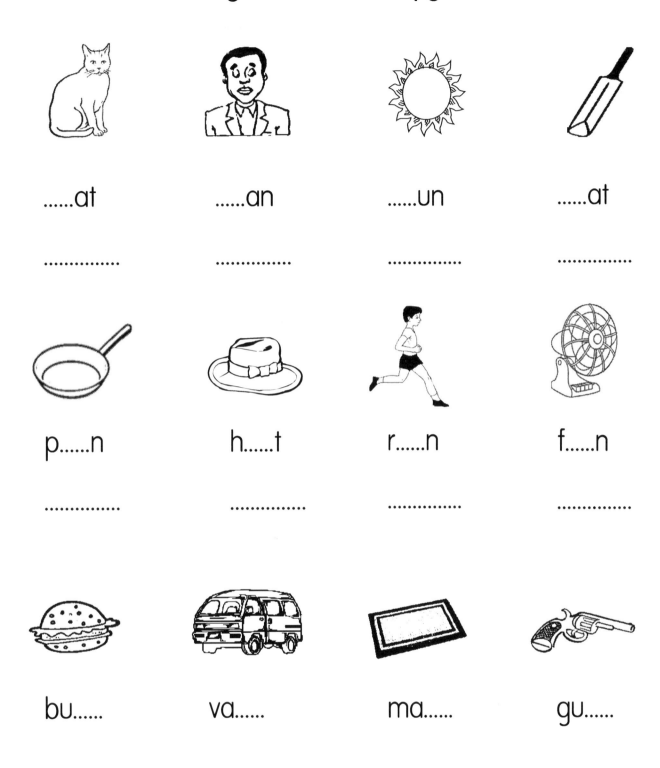

......at

......an

......un

......at

....

....

....

....

p......n

h.....t

r......n

f......n

....

....

....

....

bu......

va......

ma......

gu......

....

....

....

....

Write the missing letter and copy the word.

......et

....

......en

....

......in

....

......et

....

h......n

....

f......n

....

p......t

....

t......n

....

bi......

....

ve......

....

me......

....

pi......

....

✿ Write the word for the picture in the boxes.

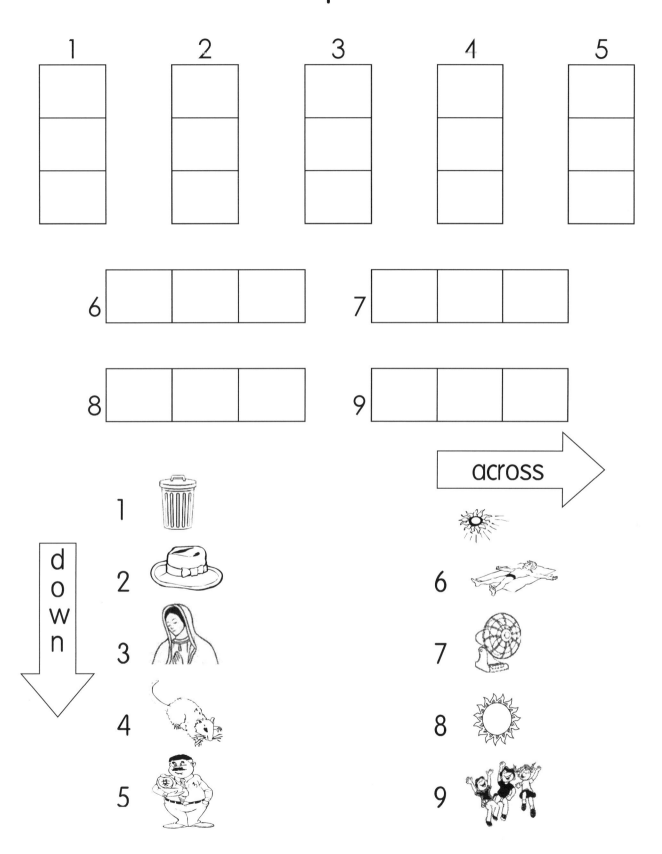

1   2   3   4   5

6   7

8   9

across →

down ↓

1

2

3

4

5

6

7

8

9

Write the word for the picture in the boxes.

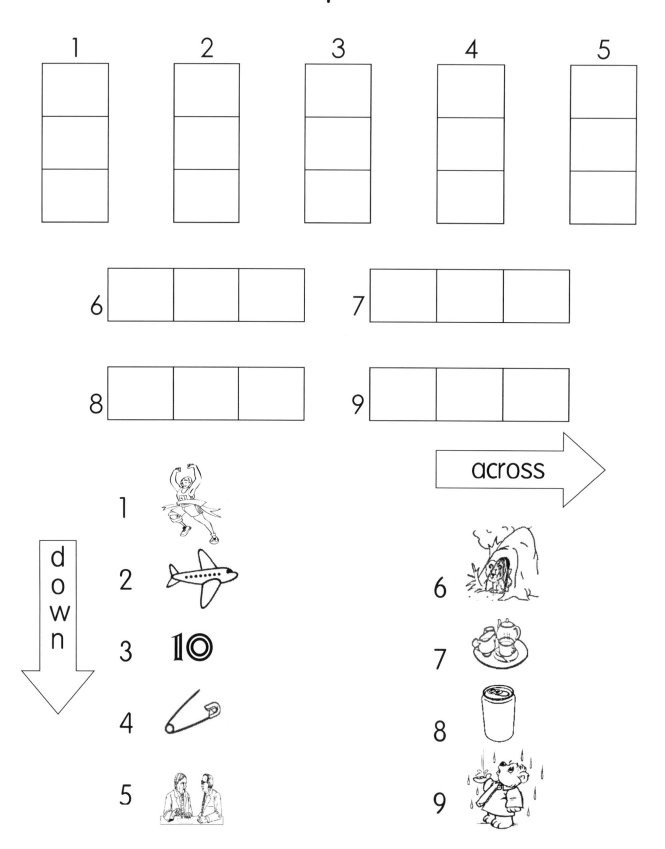

Test 1

Marks/ 40	Percent

Name: ....

1) Match the picture to the word.

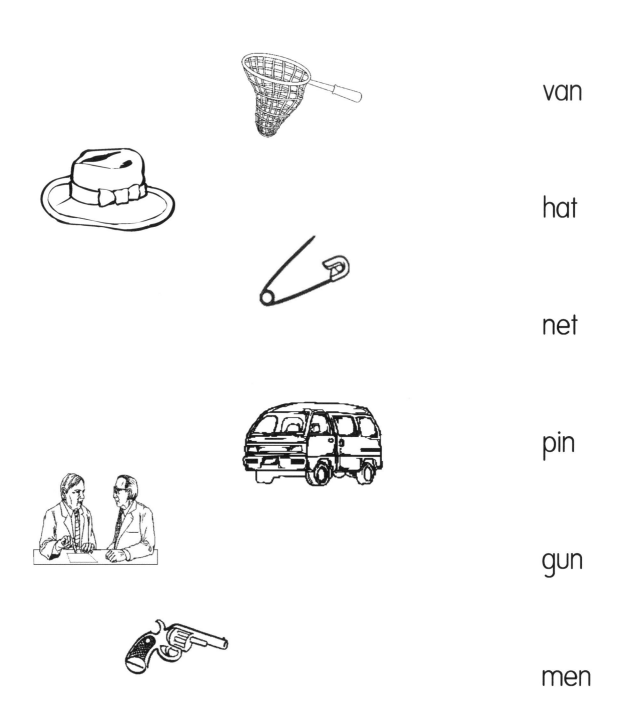

van

hat

net

pin

gun

men

2) Circle the word for the picture.

win	den	ban
fan	when	bun
ran	dot	bin
mar	sun	ten
mat	sin	tin
met	son	tan

3) Write the missing letter for the word.

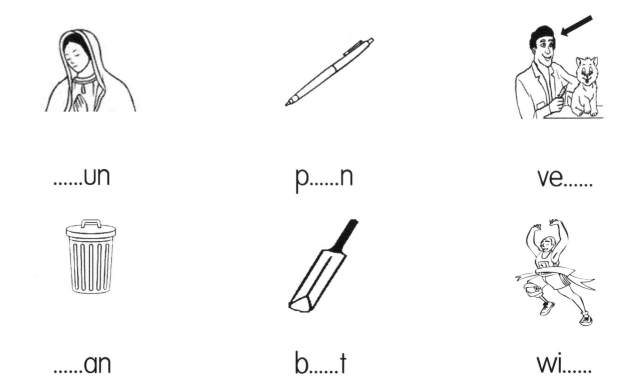

......un

p......n

ve......

......an

b......t

wi......

4) Circle a word from the brackets to complete the sentences.

1) The boy eats a (ban   bun   bin).

2) Look at the (fan   fat   pan) rat.

3) She is tall and (tin   thin   pin).

4) The (ten   then   hen) has two eggs.

5) Write the words in the correct box.

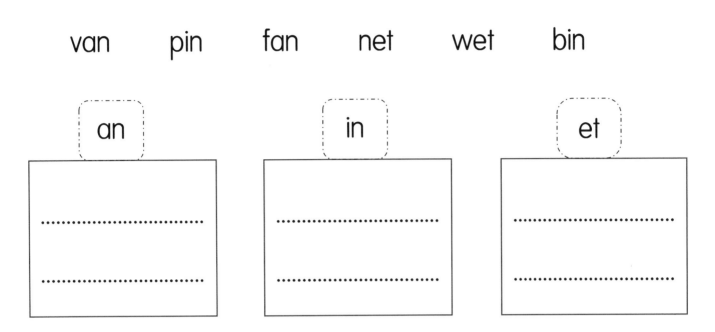

van   pin   fan   net   wet   bin

an

in

et

6) Choose a word from the box to complete the sentences.

wet   fun   men   net   hat

1) Two .... are in the van.

2) A fish is in the ....

3) The boy puts on his ....

4) The mat is ....

7) Write the word for the picture.

....

....

....

....

....

....

8) Copy each sentence and put in the word for the picture.

1) The   girl   has   a      .

....

2) Will   she   get   a   ?

....

Part 2

✿ Match the picture to the word.

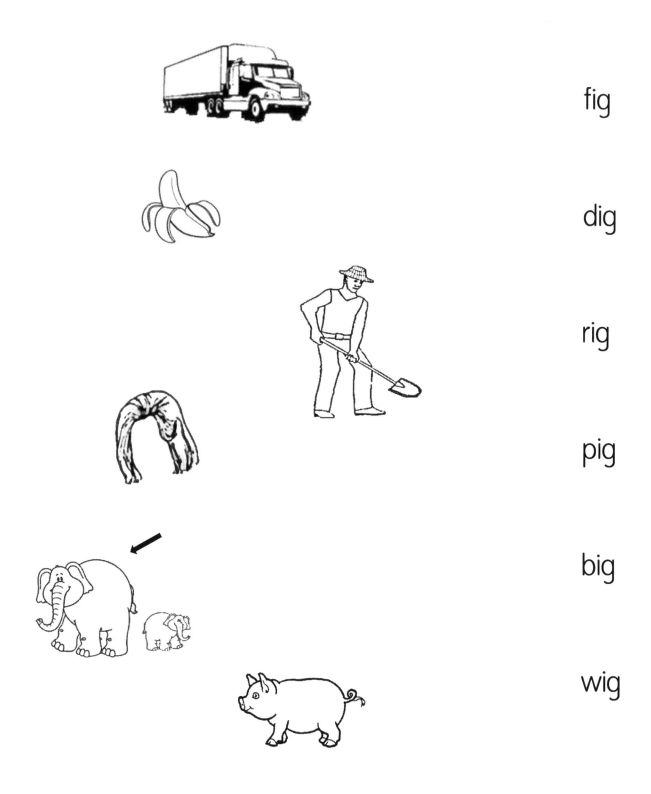

fig

dig

rig

pig

big

wig

❀ Write the word for the picture.

big   wig   pig   rig   dig   fig   jig

....

....

❀ Circle a word from the brackets to complete the sentences.

1) The (pig big wig) eats the fig.

2) Mummy wears a (dig wig rig).

3) That (dig jig rig) is very big.

✿ Match the picture to the word.

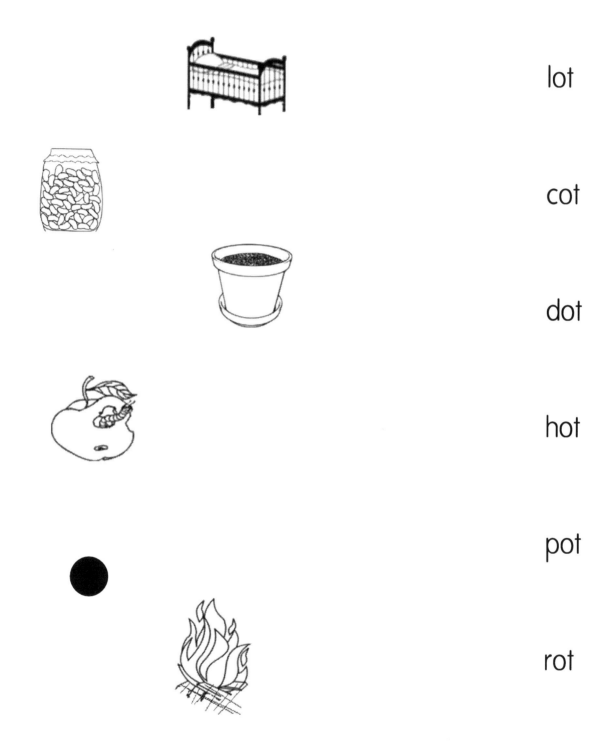

lot

cot

dot

hot

pot

rot

✿ **Write the word for the picture.**

dot   cot   hot   got   pot   rot   lot

....

....

✿ **Circle a word from the brackets to complete the sentences.**

1) The baby sleeps in the   (lot   cot   hot).

2) A flower is in the   (dot   got   pot).

3) The fire is very   (hot   rot   got).

✿ Look for the words in the boxes and circle them.

big	k b i g w d y s n g d

fig	m k c n f i g u f x c

dig	o d i g s b l c q l w

jig	r e m a t l j i g z b

pig	y t s o g b e o p i g

wig	k w i g t v l e x g f

✿ Look for the words in the boxes and circle them.

rot	x f t s r o t c n a s

lot	c l o t z k e z b r g

got	f v t w i y s x g o t

cot	u c o t a b y m e d h

dot	e t w k s f d o t x n

hot	p s d h o t e a k w d

✿ Match the picture to the word.

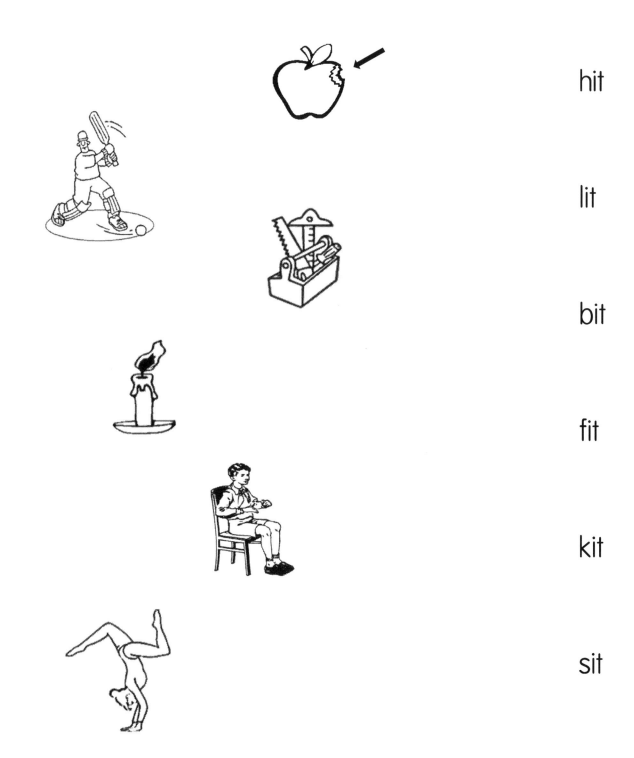

hit

lit

bit

fit

kit

sit

✿ Write the word for the picture.

hit   fit   lit   kit   bit   sit   pit

....

....

✿ Circle a word from the brackets to complete the sentences.

1) Did he (hit   bit   kit) the ball?

2) The candle was not (pit   lit   sit).

3) Will you (sit   bit   lit) on the chair?

❀ Match the picture to the word.

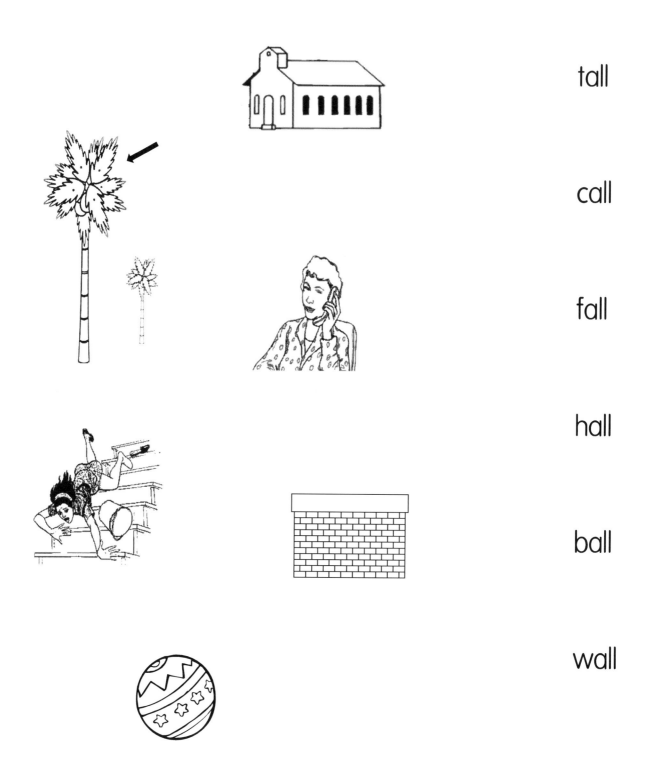

tall

call

fall

hall

ball

wall

44

❀ Write the word for the picture.

tall   call   fall   hall   ball   wall   mall

....

....

❀ Now choose a word from above to complete the sentences.

1) He plays with a big ....

2) A bird is on the ....

3) That girl is very ....

4) Did the rain ....?

45

✤ Look for the words in the boxes and circle them.

bit	b h w b i t f g n f v

fit	k f j u o h f i t x o

sit	s o h s i t x z q l x

pit	v e p a y s i g p i t

lit	l r l i t b y a t i g

kit	b k y a z y n k i t m

✿ Look for the words in the boxes and circle them.

| ball | b u r o e b a l l j h |

| fall | f y f a l l o z b s i |

| mall | v m t r s f r m a l l |

| tall | s t t a l l x m o b u |

| wall | w t v w a l l k n q w |

| call | c e c o m h b c a l l |

✿ Match the picture to the word.

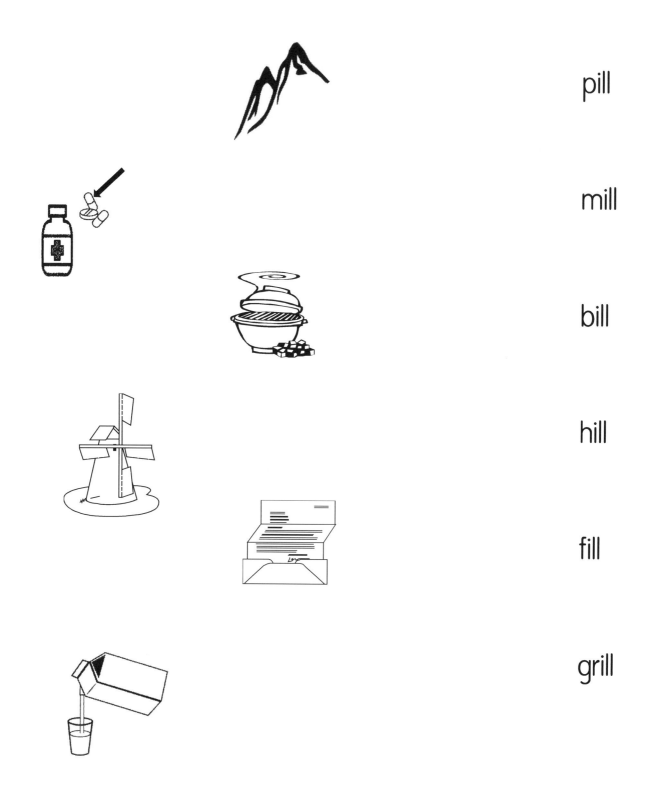

pill

mill

bill

hill

fill

grill

48

✤ **Write the word for the picture.**

fill   bill   grill   mill   will   hill   pill

....

✤ **Now choose a word from above to complete the sentences.**

1) Mummy pays the ....

2) Did you .... the jug?

3) Jack and Jill went up the ....

4) Put the meat on the ....

5) Daddy will take a ....

✿ Match the picture to the word.

yell

bell

well

sell

tell

fell

❀ **Write the word for the picture.**

well   bell   fell   tell   yell   hell   sell

....

❀ **Now choose a word from above to complete the sentences.**

1) He rings the ....

2) Water is in the ....

3) The cat .... from the tree.

4) Did you .... mummy?

5) Will the man .... the rig?

51

✿ Look for the words in the boxes and circle them.

bill	b e a b i l l s n y u
will	m w i k r w i l l s a
fill	f i h z f i l l l k h
pill	p a p i r w s p i l l
mill	y m i o g m i l l h g
hill	h i b k h i l l x d s

✿ Look for the words in the boxes and circle them.

| sell | s e v m s e l l n r k |

| hell | c h e k p h e l l x c |

| bell | b z b e w q o b e l l |

| tell | u k t e l l x m o e t |

| yell | y e w y x y e l l p k |

| fell | f s f e o h j f e l l |

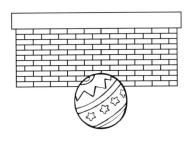

Revision 2

✿ **Write the words in the correct box.**

lit	dot	fig	jig	got
bit	sit	wig	lot	kit
pig	pit	cot	rot	big

ot	ig	it
....	....	....
....	....	....
....	....	....
....	....	....
....	....	....

✿ Write the words in the correct box.

fill   call   fall   yell   hell

pill   mill   hall   will   bell

sell   mall   fell   grill   tall

all

ell

ill

✿ Write the missing letter and copy the word.

......ot

......ig

......it

......ot

....

....

....

....

c.....t

h.....t

r.....t

p.....g

....

....

....

....

ki......

di......

fi......

si......

....

....

....

....

✿ Write the missing letter and copy the word.

......all

......ell

......ill

......all

....

....

....

....

b......ll

h......ll

f......ll

t......ll

....

....

....

....

pil......

bal......

wel......

bil......

....

....

....

....

59

✿ Write the word for the picture in the boxes.

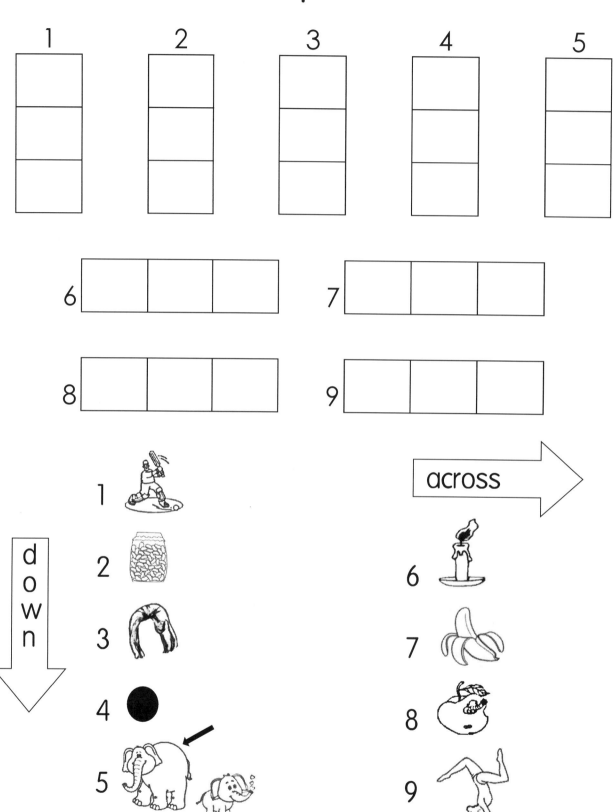

1 2 3 4 5

6 7

8 9

down →

across →

1
2
3
4
5

6
7
8
9

60

✿ Write the word for the picture in the boxes.

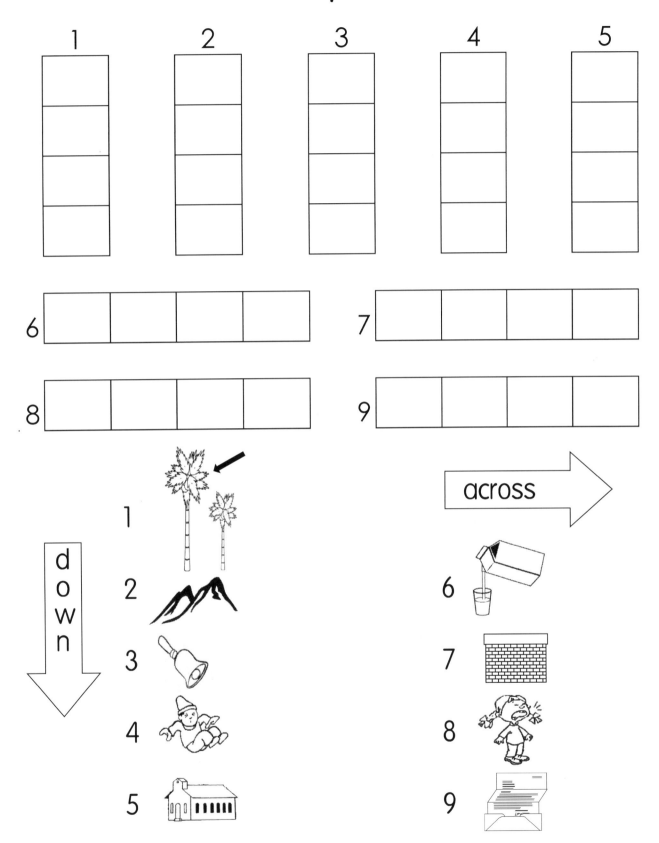

Test 2

Marks/ 40	Percent

Name: ....

1) Match the picture to the word.

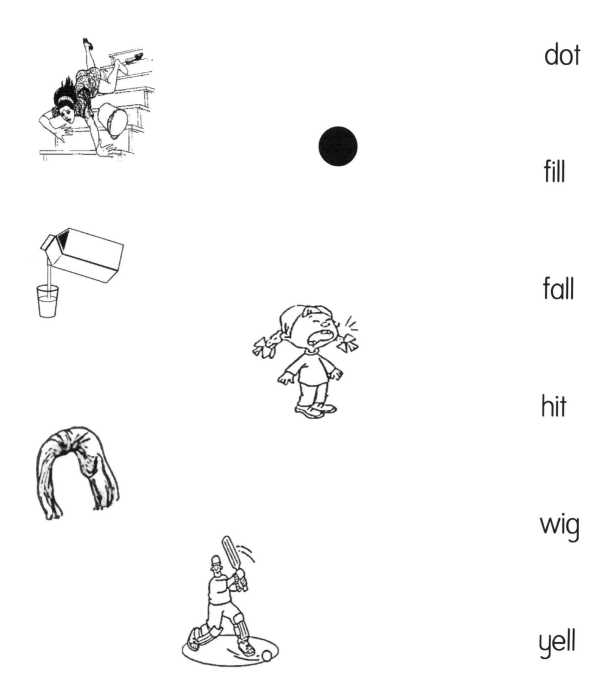

dot

fill

fall

hit

wig

yell

2) Circle the word for the picture.

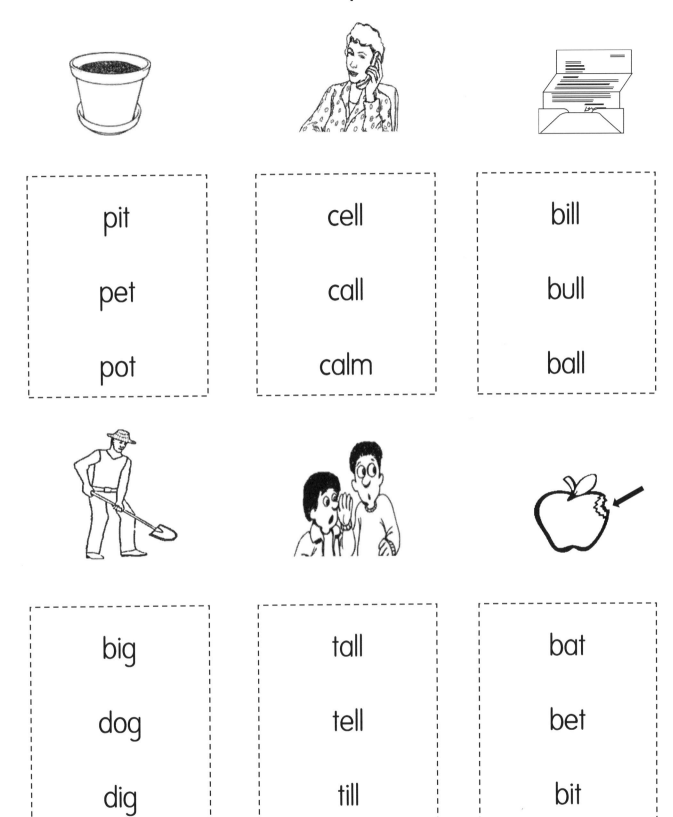

pit	cell	bill
pet	call	bull
pot	calm	ball

big	tall	bat
dog	tell	bet
dig	till	bit

65

3) Write the missing letter for the word.

......it   h......ll   ho......

......ell   gr......ll   fi......

4) Circle a word from the brackets to complete the sentences.

1) Daddy has a tool (pit   kit   hit).

2) Did she (tell   bell   yell) at you?

3) She has a (lot   rot   dot) of eggs.

4) Will he (call   sell   cell) the rig?

5) Write the words in the correct box.

rig   pit   wig   not   lot   bit

ig	ot	it
....	....	....
....	....	....

6) Choose a word from the box to complete the sentences.

tall   sell   ball   bell   hill

1) The tree is very ....

2) Will you ring the ....?

3) She plays with a little ....

4) Did she run up the ....?

7) Write the word for the picture.

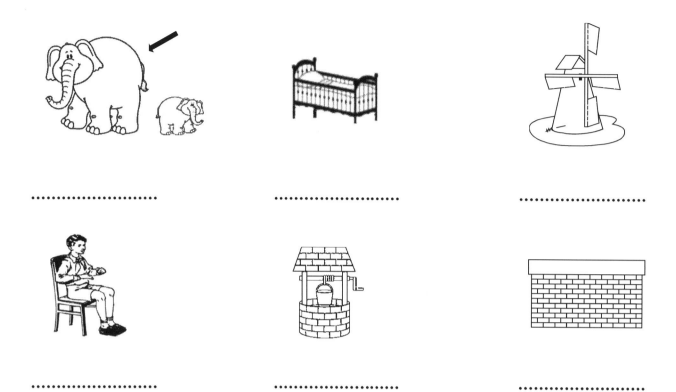

....

....

8) Copy each sentence and put in the word for the picture.

1) The   girl   is   very   .

....

2) The   is   fat.

....

Rhyme Time

✿ Words which rhyme have the same sound at the end. Match the words that rhyme.

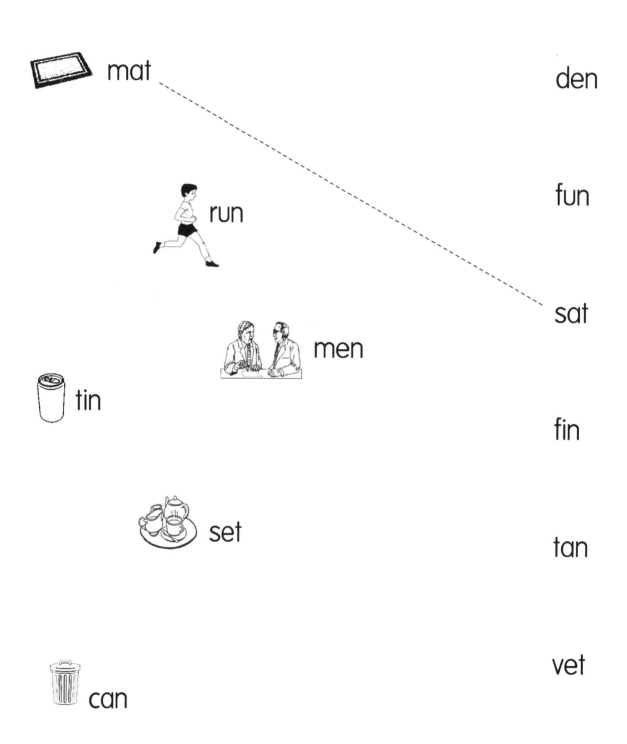

mat

run

men

tin

set

can

den

fun

sat

fin

tan

vet

✿ In each line, circle the word that rhymes with the first one.

cat	see	(rat)	car
ran	fan	ram	fun
10 ten	tin	nut	hen
wet	eat	jet	web
bun	bus	bar	sun
bin	big	win	bag

✾ Circle the two words that rhyme in each box.

Example:

ban (bat) bag (hat)

van vat can car

pet pin fin pan

nun fat nut gun

set sat met sit

man net men ten

Write two other words that rhyme with the one in the box.

cat

pan

hen

✽ Write two other words that rhyme with the one in the box.

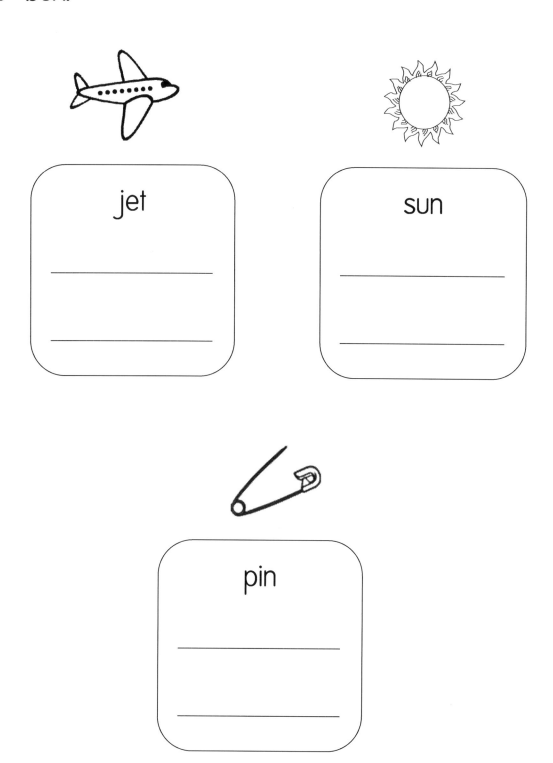

jet

_____

_____

sun

_____

_____

pin

_____

_____

74

✿ Match the words that rhyme.

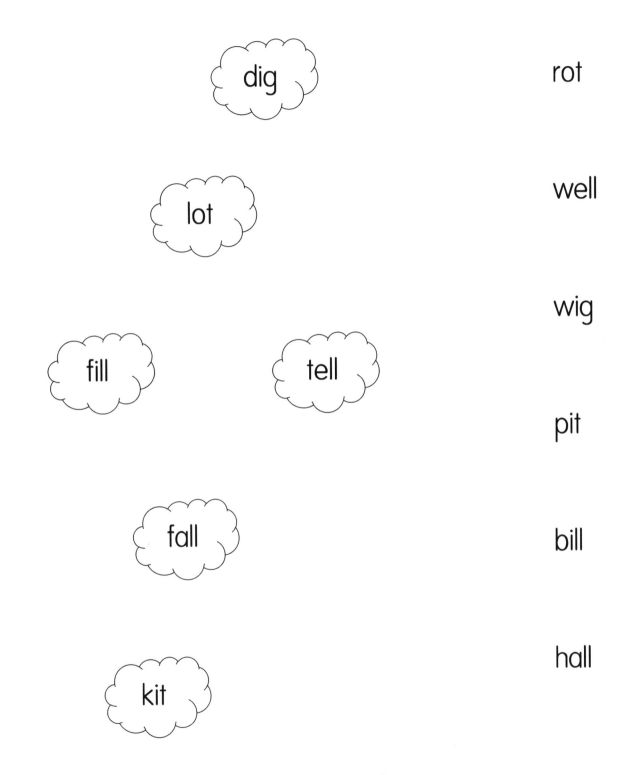

dig

lot

fill   tell

fall

kit

rot

well

wig

pit

bill

hall

75

✤ In each line, circle the word that rhymes with the first one.

fig	fin	fat	pig
cot	cat	pot	cow
sit	fit	set	fan
call	can	wall	cell
pill	mill	pin	pan
bell	ball	bed	tell

✾ Circle the two words that rhyme in each box.

dog   dot   got   gut

big   bin   bit   jig

hit   fat   fit   fig

malt   bell   ball   mall

bell   bill   bile   kill

sell   self   hell   hall

✿ Write two other words that rhyme with the one in the box.

pig

_____

_____

pot

_____

_____

lit

_____

_____

78

✿ Write two other words that rhyme with the one in the box.

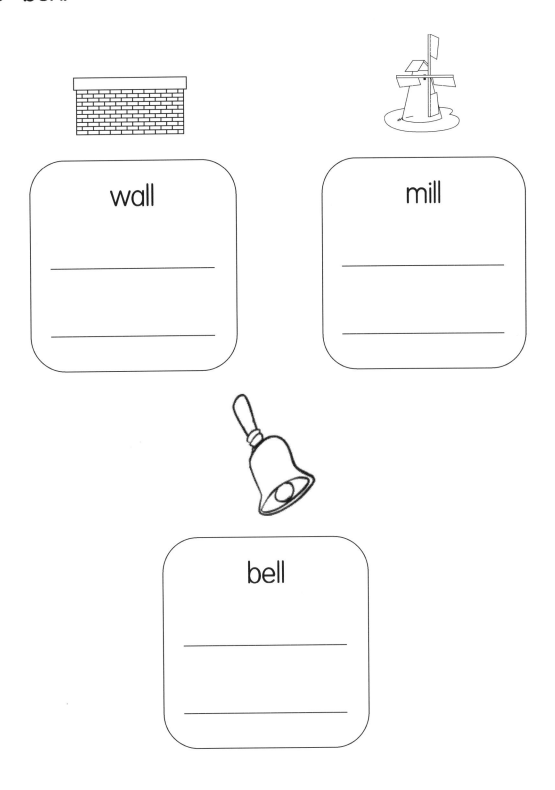

wall

_____

_____

mill

_____

_____

bell

_____

_____

79

Words to Learn

1	2	3	4
bat	ban	den	get
cat	can	hen	jet
fat	fan	men	net
hat	man	pen	pet
mat	pan	ten	set
rat	tan	then	vet
vat	van	when	wet

5	6	7	8
bun	bin	big	cot
fun	fin	dig	dot
gun	pin	fig	got
pun	sin	jig	hot
nun	tin	pig	lot
run	thin	rig	pot
sun	win	wig	rot

9	10	11	12
bit	ball	bill	bell
fit	call	fill	fell
hit	fall	grill	hell
kit	hall	hill	sell
lit	mall	mill	tell
pit	tall	pill	well
sit	wall	will	yell

Homework

	Page / Pages		Page / Pages
1		21	
2		22	
3		23	
4		24	
5		25	
6		26	
7		27	
8		28	
9		29	
10		30	
11		31	
12		32	
13		33	
14		34	
15		35	
16		36	
17		37	
18		38	
19		39	
20		40	

Made in the USA
Columbia, SC
23 April 2022